3 Day Guide to Prague

A 72-hour definitive guide on what to see, eat and enjoy in Prague,

Czech Republic

3 DAY CITY GUIDES

Cover Images

Cover Photo Credits:

Prazsky orloj. Photo by George M. Groutas

Prague. Photo by Jörg Schubert

Prague, Czech Republic. Photo by Thomas Depenbusch

Prague seen from Letna Park. Photo by Roman Boed

ISBN: 1512042773
ISBN-13: 978-1512042771

"The journey is the destination." — *Dan Eldon*

CONTENTS

1 INTRODUCTION TO PRAGUE

Prague embankment in one beautiful summer evening. Photo by <u>Jan Fidler</u>

Prague – the beauty of this city coupled with its renowned (and cheap) selection of beer brings travelers from around the world. It's easy to fall in love with the eternal beauty of Staré město (Old Town), an almost fairytale like setting that looks as though it's been left behind in Medieval times. As you walk through Prague, you will find that it's never predictable. You will see Gothic structures and spires, charming parks, cobble-stone streets, beautiful bridges, elegant cathedrals, imposing palaces, buzzing beer gardens and pubs, lively street shows, quiet cafes, and historic theaters.

Prague has a lively entertainment scene, with venues that offer it all, from local to international artists, and is a host to a very happening nightlife scene in Europe. Prague is also home to several music festivals such as the Prague International Jazz Festival. The city is also known for its museums, the most notable is National Museum, housing various pieces of art, music, and natural history in multiple buildings that are dotted throughout the city.

The charm of Prague entices directors and location scouts to shoot films and music videos in the area: some of the more notable films shot in the area include: Mission Impossible, EuroTrip, Narnia, and Van Helsing. With its imprint in film and cinema, it is no wonder that Prague also hosts a variety of annual international film festivals such as the One World Film Festival, and a taste of the Karlovy Vary International Film Festival.

Of all the famous cities of Europe, Prague is one of the most economical with respect to food and lodging. It has the charm of Paris, but without the inflated price tag. Speaking of money, while the Czech Republic belongs to the European Union, they do not use the Euro as their official currency. They use Czech koruna (CZK); however, some stores do accept the euro as a form of payment.

Shopping in Prague is a delight as it has something for everyone. Prague is most noted for the *antikvariats* which are used, antique books or printed material. The prices vary depending on the type of book that you are looking for, and some of these antikvariats offer books in several languages. Other souvenirs that you can take home: Czech garnets. Although technically available throughout the whole of the Czech Republic, these gems are exquisite, dark red stones. You can easily pick these up from various jewelry stores (klenoty) in the area.

Prague also has various shopping malls that you can visit; the grandest being the Palladium, just a few minutes from the Old Town Square. It houses several international brands that you may get back home, as well as local stores that you can discover. Before you leave Prague, be sure to also check out some of the handmade wooden toys (hracky).

Prague is extraordinary but also a city with enough international familiarity that new travellers will feel comfortable touring in. It will undoubtedly push you out of your comfort zone but offers enough international familiarity that you won't feel like a fish out of water. Now that you have a dipped your feet in the basics of Prague, it's time to dive deeper into the details of the city, and how to best plan your stay.

History

Prague is also known as "Praha" and is the capital of the Czech Republic (a country known before 1993 as Czechoslovakia). It is the capital of the Bohemia region and used to be a part of the vast

Austro-Hungarian Empire. This is a capital that has been occupied since 5500BC, with the most notable residents arriving in the 6th century, the Slavs, which have been the most dominant ethnic group ever since.

It was said that the beginnings of Prague can be traced from a princess named Libuse, who married a man named Premsyl and has since founded the Premsyl Dynasty. Prince Wenceslas, a descendant from the Premsyl dynasty, is the most beloved patron saint of the area (Bohemia), and is also referenced in a popular Christmas Song – "Good King Wenceslas" – as he was assassinated when he was campaigning for Bohemia to have equal rights in Great Moravia. There were many other rulers after him, but the city had its renaissance during the 14th Century, during the reign of Charles IV.

The king helped Prague become the third most populated city in Europe and became the capital of the Holy Roman Empire in 1315. He founded Charles Bridge, New Town, and St Vitus Cathedral. With his efforts, he also spearheaded the rebuilding of Prague Cathedral, and introduced a new style of art called the "Bohemian School," and thus, the Czech Republic became one of the most powerful countries in Europe during his reign.

In 1867, Emperor Francis Joseph I established the Austro-Hungarian Empire, which was then defeated during World War I and led to the creation of the country Czechoslovakia, with Prague chosen as the capital of the newly formed country. Prague had a German-speaking majority in the 19th century, but that majority soon declined in number and influence and Prague became majority Czech-speaking in late 19th century.

From 1939, Nazi Germany took over Czechoslovakia, where the citizens of Prague were oppressed by the Nazis. The city was bombed, leaving large parts of the city damaged or destroyed. On May 8, 1945, the Germans finally left Prague, as the Soviets came to liberate the city from the Germans, only to secede again under the Soviets.

In 1968, the city was invaded by Soviet Union tanks, designed to stop the spreading of the "Socialism with a human face" concept engineered by its popular and charismatic leader, Alexander Dubcek. This event came to be known as "Prague Spring."

Finally, in 1989, during the fall of the Berlin Wall, Czechoslovakia was liberated from communism and the Soviets, becoming its own separate country. In 1993, under the peaceful split of the countries of Czech Republic & Slovakia, Prague became the official capital of the Czech Republic.

Prague is the fifth most visited European city due to its history, cultural landmarks, lively atmosphere, efficient public transport, and, of course, legendary beer.

Climate and seasons

Prague has four seasons:

Winter:

December – February; winter can be brutal with snow and below zero temperatures. Average temperatures range between 0 to -5 degrees Celsius (30-37 Fahrenheit); snow can be expected, with an average of 3-8 inches. Despite the chill, winter can be a fun time to visit. It's the time when the Christmas Markets begin popping up and you can buy food and other wares from the market. It is also a good time to take advantage of off-peak rates for pretty much anything. The sun sets earlier than the other seasons, making the ambiance a little greyer, and some attractions are closed or have limited operating hours, so plan accordingly. Bring those thick coats, boots, and warmers, if you still choose to go during this time.

Spring:

March – May, with average temperatures between 10 and 20 Celsius (50 and 67 Fahrenheit). The weather can be a bit milder than winter, but during March, you may still get bouts of snowfall here and there. Still bring coats and boots to pack, but you will begin to see growth on the trees throughout the parks – flowers start to bloom and the trees begin growing their leaves back.

Summer:

June – August; with average temperatures between 20 and 30 Celsius (67 and 87 Fahrenheit). Prague experiences nice, warm summers, and also hot days. If you plan to go, bring clothes that you can layer. Summer in Prague, on average, also gets the most rainfall out of the other times of the year so the weather may change from warm to cool within a span of a few hours. Depending on your heat tolerance, the summers can be lighter than compared to countries with a more tropical climate. This is the most crowded time of the year, but you can expect that the attractions you want to visit has longer operating hours as compared to the rest of the year.

Fall:

September – November, with average temperatures between 7 and 17 Celsius (44 and 62 Fahrenheit). The weather starts to cool down a bit more from the summer, and most of the tourists leave and the locals come back from their summer holidays. Pack your jacket, as it may get cold, but not cold enough for a winter jacket just yet. The leaves begin to fall from the trees, making this a good time to spend the afternoon playing or kicking them around in the parks. Most leaves change from green to red or brown, making for a surreal photo experience.

Best Time to Visit

The best time to visit this side of the world is during late spring (late April – May) or early autumn (late

September – early November). The weather is not as scorching hot as summer, and is actually quite pleasant. The spring time includes lively festivals and celebrations, such as the Easter Market.

Prague is also a good place to visit during winter (if you can stand the cold and the snow), simply for their winter market and a smaller amount of tourists. During this time of the year, you don't compete with other tourists for space at some of the most popular sites, nor do you pay as much for hotels and other tours.

For the film buffs, a exciting time to visit is in July, when the Karlovy Vary Film Festival is in full swing, held in the charming Karlovy Vary (90 mins away by car), a town famous for spas and visiting movie stars.

Language

The official language in Prague is Czech. The Czech and Slovak languages are almost the same (stemming back from their history as one country – Czechoslovakia), but the main difference is how the Czechs and the Slovaks spell and enunciate certain words. Their language is not the easiest to learn (it comes from the Slavic tradition and is not the same or similar to Russian, which is a common mistake people make when they first hear the language), and nor is it easy to speak (the spelling and how they pronounce a word could be completely different from each other). The city's signs are mostly written in Czech.

Here are useful informative words and phrases for use during your trip:

Ahoj (pronounced: Ahoy) – Hello

Kde je banka? (Gedye ye banka) – Where is the bank?

Prepáčte, mluvíte Anglicky (Prepachte mlouveete Anglitski)? – Excuse me, do you speak English?

Kde je metro? (Gedye ye metro) – Where is the metro?

Pivo – Beer

Pomoc (Pomots) – Help

Getting In:

Prague has an international airport called "Vaclav Havel." Multiple airlines land here, some budget (like EasyJet, WizzAir, among others), and legacy carriers (British Airways, Lufthansa, KLM, Delta). It is the hub of Czech Airlines, the national airline of the Czech Republic. With multiple airline connections from various airline partners, it is very easy to fly to Prague. It is approximately 43 minutes using public transportation using a combination of buses, trams, and the metro; and approximately 20 minutes if you are taking a taxi or other private transportation from the airport to the Old Town, where most tourists flock to.

Alternatively, you can take a train from pretty much anywhere in Europe to Prague. The main train station is called "Praha" – Hlavní Nádraží (Prague – Main Station).

The two other important stations are Nádraží Holešovice (Holešovice Station) and Nádraží Smíchov (Smíchov Station).

There are three main railways: Czech Railways (České Dráhy), RegioJet, and Leo Express. Czech Railways covers more routes, but RegioJet and Leo Express offer good service at comparable prices and are newer additions to the Czech Train Transport world.

http://www.le.cz/index.php

https://jizdenky.studentagency.cz/?1

https://www.cd.cz/en/default.htm

Another way to arrive in Prague is by a river cruise from Europe – these normally ply the Danube River, but to actually get to Prague from your port of call, you will need to transfer using a bus or the train.

Getting around:

There are several ways of getting around the city:

Metro - The first is using the extensive and well-designed metro, which will take you around the entire city at reasonable prices. It currently has three lines (with a fourth still being constructed), which can take you pretty much anywhere you need to go in the city. Download a map in advance to get yourself acquainted with transfer points and gain a feel of the stations that are closest to the stops you want to visit. http://www.dpp.cz/download-file/3690/metro_trams_A4_en.pdf

Bus (Autobus) – The buses are plentiful and offer a cheap, easy, and safe way to get around the city. Tickets can be bought at various locations around the city, including newsstands. The downside of buses is that you may get lost as compared to the metro or the tram, and some of the routes change depending on what time you board in the evening. Any bus marked with an M means that you can connect to a metro using that particular bus route. Buy a ticket if you don't have the Prague pass then validate it immediately upon boarding to avoid any fines from an inspector.

Taxis – Unfortunately, Prague has a bad reputation when it comes to taxis. A study concluded in July 2012 showed that only one out of five taxi drivers takes the most direct route from point A to point B and charges the correct fare. However, do not let that study dissuade you from taking a taxi in Prague if you are in a pinch, just exercise caution. These incidents generally happen if you flag a taxi from the street. Before you get into a taxi that you flag, try to haggle the price down to one you will be willing to pay (even if it is slightly above the normal tariff) – check with your hotel and ask how much normal fares are so you will know what to expect. To identify a real taxi in Prague, check for a yellow roof lamp which says TAXI on both sides. The driver's name & license number should also be printed on both the front doors of the taxi.

Reputable taxi companies in Prague and their websites:

AAA Radiotaxi - www.aaa-taxi.cz
Halotaxi - www.halotaxi.cz
Profi Taxi - www.profitaxi.cz
Sedop - www.sedop.cz

Tram (Tramvaje) – Trams don't have as wide a reach as the metro, but they offer a convenient way to travel if you happen to miss a bus. The tram looks like a hybrid of a metro and a bus but provides access to many of the places that buses can't. These trams run from day to night, with certain routes only specific to the evening. Tram 22 is the most scenic route, where you can see glimpses of the National Theatre, Prague Castle, and Belvedere (Queen Anne's Summer Palace).

Additionally, here's some useful information as you venture throughout Prague:

http://www.dpp.cz/en/ - the official site of the Prague Public Transit.

http://www.dpp.cz/en/fares-in-prague/ - If you are staying for more than three days in Prague, a 3-day transit pass will cost you about 310 CZK. The pass includes fares in trams, the metro, buses, and ferries. It will save you the hassle of deciphering the fare to different parts of the city and figuring out how much the fare price is from point A to point B.

2: PRAGUE NEIGHBORHOODS

Prague is actually quite big, if you look at the city – and after spending time here, you'll find they distinguish their districts by numbers.

What can make navigation confusing to travelers is that within each numbered district, they have names for smaller neighborhoods within the area. Here is a brief guide to get you more acquainted with the city. We'll concentrate more on the most popular districts:

Stare Mesto – The Old Town, this is the medieval settlement of Prague, settled in the early 9th century and expanded in the 14th century. Home to many famous sites like the Old Town Square, Astronomical Clock, and Synagogue.

Mala Strana – The "Little Quarter" and is touted as second only to the Old Town. The neighborhood is situated on the left bank of the River Vltava, and below Prague Castle, across Charles Bridge from the Old Town. Originally called "New Town beneath Prague Castle" in the 13th century, until it was renamed in the 17th century.

Josefov – Called the "Jewish Quarters" and it is the smallest area within Prague, completely surrounded by the Old Town. Known for the narrow streets, where you will find sights such as Kafka's birthplace, the Old Jewish Cemetery, and several Synagogues you may visit.

Nove Mesto – Literal meaning: "New Town" but still considered as part of the historic center of Prague. Founded by Charles IV as an extension from the Old Town. Here you'll find Wenceslas Square and the New Town Hall.

*Note: the above four are in **Prague District 1**. Staying in District 1 means you're paying for a premium as it's the most beautiful and historic part of the city. Other recommended neighborhoods are:

Vinohrady (Prague 2/3/4/10) – Literally named vineyards because the land used to be vineyards in the 14th century. Home to a lot of parks, but the area is the second most expensive area after Prague 1.

Zizkov (Prague 3) – Mostly a residential suburb but home to various expats. Named after the military leader Jan Zizka. It is here you'll find Vitkov Hill, where the Battle of Vitkov Hill occured – it was a turning point for Prague in the 15th century when they defeated the Roman forces. Within this district, you'll find the Zizkov TV Tower and various monuments to heroes past.

Vysehrad (Prague 2) – Known as "upper castle"

and is the home of the historic fort in the city.

Walking Tours

New Prague Tours is a company that offers free walking tours of Prague. The way it works is they guide you around the area, and after the tour, you tip your guide whatever amount you deem fit. A great way to see the city without spending much money. No need for a pre-booking either: you just show up at the meeting area 10-15 minutes before the tour leaves and you're in!
http://www.newpraguetours.com/

Prague Tours by Segway - great for those who don't like walking and want the novelty of riding a Segway on the historic streets.
http://www.pragueonsegway.com/

Discover Prague: Royal Walk Free Tour – offering premium & free tours, the free tour is 2 ½ hours long, and no pre-booking required.
http://www.discover-prague.com/en/tour/3/royal-walk-free-tour

3: HOW NOT TO GET LOST IN PRAGUE

Prague is a city with 10 districts- now how do you not get lost wandering around all these districts? Here's a little guide that can hopefully help you find your way around. Prague isn't an easy city to get around in, as the signs are in Czech and its narrow roads may start to look alike after you have walked around for a while.

You can use a few reference points in the hopes of helping you to not get lost:

The River Vltava – The River can be a good guiding point across the city. To navigate to the city center, try looking for bridges or other signs that may say Stare Mesto (which means Old Town). Once you see Charles Bridge, you know that you are downtown. On one end of the bridge is Mala Strana, the other is Stare Mesto.

Look at the landmarks – if you see Prague Castle towering above you, walk near the bottom of it and you'll get to Mala Strana. If you are on the hill (within close distance to Prague Castle), you are in Hradcany (the castle district). The avenue from Wenceslas Square (Vaclavske nam) stretches southeast from Stare Mesto to the National

Museum, and ends at the main train station. Those are the main areas that you are probably going to go around in, otherwise, if you find yourself in another district of Prague, look for a tram stop and find a map from there. See if it goes back to Stare Mesto or the train station and work your way from there to get your bearings as necessary.

Tourist Information Centers are great as well for finding your way around. You can find them at the following locations below and are marked with a white "i" sign with a green box behind it. The airport location is the easiest one to access if you have just flown in and have no clue where to go.

Prague Airport – Terminal 1 (9AM-7PM)

Prague Airport – Terminal 2 (8AM-8PM)

Old Town Hall - Staroměstské náměstí 1, Praha 1 - Staré Město (9AM-7PM). Centrally located in Old Town, you can also use this as a place to buy the Prague card, tours & other events, or to ask for suggestions where to go if lost or don't know which activity to hit.

Rytířská Street, Rytířská 31, Praha 1 - Staré Město (10AM-6PM) – Also in the Old Town, next to the Estates Theatre.

Wenceslas Square, Václavské náměstí (roh se Štěpánskou ulicí), Praha 1 - Nové Město (10AM-6PM). Located in the New Town, right in the middle of Wenceslas Square.

Lesser Town (Mala Strana) Bridge Tower (open only from April to October, 10AM-6PM) – directly under the tower, this information desk is easy to find!

Other conventional means of getting around & finding your way:

Google Maps – Did you know that saying "Ok Maps" the map area you were looking at will be preloaded in the cache of your device? Use this feature when you want to find your way around the old town and through Mala Strana. It will save you so much time when trying to figure out the streets.

Paper Maps – Feeling really lost? Grab a paper map from the tourist information office. They provide more detail than the ones you can find in the free brochures.

Asking directions - You can ask locals where to go by saying *Kde je* (location) (example: *Gedye ye Stare Mesto*) – "Where is_____?"

4 DAY 1 IN PRAGUE

The first day in Prague is a great opportunity to explore the beautiful Old Town (Stare Mesto). It is very walkable, so while there are many places to visit, take time to soak in the atmosphere of Prague and feel the air, so to speak. To get you further acquainted with the city, the Old Town is in Prague 1 and is bordered by the streets Revoluční, Na Příkopě, and Národni.

To start your day, consider going to **Café Imperial** or **Café Louvre** for a filling and delicious breakfast. Café Imperial is just a block away from the Namesty Republiky station and is very close to the Hilton Prague Old Town or the Marriott. Meanwhile, Café Louvre is a quick 9 minute walk away from the Old Town. Assuming you start off from your hotel at 7:30/8:00AM, budget around an hour for breakfast, and you'll be out and ready to go by 9:00AM at the latest.

http://www.cafelouvre.cz/en/Offer/breakfast/

Open 8am – 11:30 p.m.

http://cafeimperial.cz/en/food

Open 7am – 11 p.m.

Bethlehem Chapel. Photo by <u>Wolfgang Sauber</u>

If you chose to eat at Café Louvre, it is worth stopping by the **Bethlehem Chapel** (Betlémská kaple), a medieval chapel founded in 1391. While the chapel is simple, it is considered a national cultural monument. You can linger peacefully in the chapel to view the paintings and layout of the building. However, if it is closed, you can readily take photos outside the chapel.

http://www.bethlehemchapel.eu

Open from 10:00AM to 6:00PM daily.

From the Bethlehem Chapel or your breakfast at Café Imperial, your next stop should be to visit the **Old Town Square**. If you're lucky, you might see street performers in action, performing funny battle scenes, and be sure to check out the various shops and vendors on display. The square has come a long way from its macabre past when the square was used for town executions. However it still draws its share of riotous crowds, especially when it comes to ice hockey celebrations. If you arrive between 9:15-9:30AM, you will have a few minutes to watch the people in the square, but if not, head straight to the clock.

Old Music in Prague. Photo by <u>Roman Boed</u>

of the most striking traditions of Old Town happens at the top of every hour, when the **"Walk of the Apostles"** *happens every hour, every single day.* It is a delightful show of colorful figurines at the top of the **Astronomical Clock Orloj**. The Orloj is the oldest astronomical clock in the world that's still working. *It is open 24/7 every single day.* The apostles who come out of the clock were carved by a marionette artist, Vojtech Sucharda as a replacement for the destroyed marionettes from 1945. At the end of the apostles, you will find death, striking time, so the walk is a must see, simply for its history.

Prazsky orloj. Photo by <u>George M. Groutas</u>

You can find this clock at the **Old Town Hall** and note that you may be looking up for some time at the clock so best be prepared. Try arriving at least 10 minutes before the clock goes off so you can get a good spot to view the clock. *The whole walk of the apostles' experience lasts around 5 minutes.* If you manage to watch the 10:00AM show, you can head inside the Old Town Hall immediately after and do the guided tour of the East Wing, showcasing the tower, underground areas, and the historic halls. Entrance is 120 CZK for adults, discounted fees apply for children.

http://www.staromestskaradnicepraha.cz/

http://www.prague.eu/en/object/places/188/old-town-hall-with-astronomical-clock-staromestska-radnice-s-orlojem?back=1

Open from 11:00AM – 10:00PM.

You'll probably be hungry and craving lunch after the tower tour, so stop by **Restaurace Mlejnice,** a quick 5 minute walk from the Old Town Square. Budget a maximum of two hours to enjoy your lunch and a drink from their extensive wine and whiskey collection before you move on to your next attraction.

http://www.restaurace-mlejnice.cz/en/index.html

Žatecká 17 Josefov 110 00 Praha

Open from 11:00AM – 11:30PM.

There's no better way to shed those lunch calories than by a lovely stroll to the historic **Charles Bridge (**Karlův mos), *open 24 hours – a pedestrian-only bridge.* Charles Bridge is an easy 9-15 minute walk (depending how fit you or your companions are) from the restaurant (700 meters). It is a historic arch bridge that has 16 arches, three bridge towers, and several statues that line the bridge. These statues that you see on the bridge are replicas of the originals that were sculpted in 1700, the most famous of which being St Luthgard, St

John of Nepomuk, and the Holy Crucifix of Calvary.

Charles Bridge. Photo by <u>Roman Boed</u>

Allot around an hour max to walk across the bridge and take photos of the statues. For an enhanced experience, you can take a relaxed, fun, and informative **Charles Bridge boat tour** on the Vltava River, which sails underneath the Charles Bridge and gives you a fantastic view of some of Prague's most famous landmarks. The cruise departs at 3:00PM or 4:00PM (depending on your speed for lunch or your walk across Charles Bridge. You can either choose the 3pm or the 4pm boat departure), and the tour should *last for an hour* for 190 CZK.

http://www.cruise-prague.cz/cruises

If you finished the boat tour at 5:00PM, you'll find that most of the tourist attractions are closed for admissions at this time. However it's a great time to wander and explore the streets for shops that may still be open while taking in the beautiful architecture that the *Old Town* has to offer. There are several interesting buildings within this quarter, many of which are not tourist attractions themselves but provide and inviting gaze into the past, all the same. At this time you may opt to have an early dinner in the city, or head to your hotel directly to relax and prepare for another early day in Prague.

5 DAY 2 IN PRAGUE

Today, you will begin by discovering the district of **Hradcany**, also known as the castle district of Prague. For breakfast, head to *Terasa U Zlate Studne* (see deluxe dining below for more information). *Open from 7:00AM to 11:00PM*.

http://www.terasauzlatestudne.cz/en/

Prague Castle. Photo by <u>Ricardo Liberato</u>

After breakfast, your first port of call will be **Prague Castle,** the residence of the President of the Czech Republic, and also a Guinness Book of Record holder for the largest ancient castle in the world. The biggest draw to Prague Castle would be the *Changing of the Guard* at *noon*. It's best if you get a ticket according to your needs, as there are multiple circuits you can do. For those who love history and want to see the most buildings, do Circuit A – which covers the tickets for St Vitus, the Old Royal Palace, several exhibitions, St George's Basilica, the Golden Lane with Daliborka Tower, the Powder Tower & the Rosenberg Palace (350 CZK).

Meanwhile, Circuit B is a more condensed version of circuit A, only covering entrances to St Vitus, the Royal Palace, St George's Basilica & Daliborka Tower (250 CZK). If you choose circuit A, note that this may take the around 8 hours (including a break for lunch and viewing the gardens) while circuit B will probably take around 5 hours – for this purpose, we are going to focus on Circuit A.

https://www.hrad.cz/en/prague-castle/prague-castle-tourist-information/visit-of-prague-castle.shtml

Open from 5:00AM until midnight in the summer, 6:00AM-11:00PM in the winter.

After you buy your ticket to the castle & compound, your next stop is just adjacent to the castle, **St. Vitus Cathedral (**Metropolitní katedrála svatého Víta, Václava a Vojtěcha) – this impressively built Gothic landmark is the most important Catholic Church in the country. Several Bohemian kings and notable people have been buried in its complex. You can spend two hours going around the

Cathedral and the crypt and enjoying its beauty.

Inside the Prague Cathedral. Photo by <u>Tambako The Jaguar</u> **CC BY-ND**

III. Nádvoří 48/2, 119 01 Praha 1

http://www.katedralasvatehovita.cz/en

Open from 9AM-5PM

Once you're done with St Vitus, try and catch the **Changing of the Guards** at noon, which involves fanfare and a flag ceremony. It only happens once a day, so try to catch it while you can! Best to get to the area before 12 to get a great viewing spot, and estimate around 10 minutes for the entire fanfare and experience to finish.

You can grab lunch at **Lvi Dvur,** situated inside a building that has been standing since 1521 and within the Prague castle compound. Try the Prague

Piglet for around 595 CZK. Otherwise, there are plenty of other choices from the pub menu that you can choose from.

U Prašného mostu 51/6 118 00 Praha 1

http://www.lvidvur.cz/en/index.php

Open from 11:00AM – 11:00PM

Powder Tower. Photo by <u>Brian Jeffery Beggerly</u>

You can continue your tour of the castle grounds at the **Powder Tower** – one of the original gates of the Old Town of Prague. Go up 186 steps to the viewing deck as part of your experience. Allot 30-45 minutes for this, depending on how fast you go up or down the stairs. From there, you can continue on to the other stops of the Circuit A ticket that you bought, ending at the courtyard of Prague Castle (as that closes the latest).

You can then retire to your hotel after a long day of walking in the compound or head off to one of the nightlife spots that Prague is extremely proud of.

6 DAY 3 IN PRAGUE

It's another morning of exploring and this time, we'll venture to the other side of Charles Bridge/Old Town to uncover what else it has to offer. You can start your day off at the **Café Pointa,** a new café serving pastries, croissants, sandwiches, and other yummy goodies to provide you some energy. Try their fresh butter croissant that comes with a serving of tea or get a meal if you're feeling hungry.

http://we-like-it-fresh.wix.com/cafepointa#!about/c42f

Na Valech 2, 160 00, Praha 6

Open from 9AM-9:30PM

See **Lobkowicz Palace**, another palace within the Prague Castle Complex that you may have missed out on your second day – notable for its various collections, and where you'll learn more about the Lobkowicz Palace. An audio tour is included with your entrance fee: allot around two hours to explore the palace in its entirety before you move on to watch the midday concert at the hall.

http://www.lobkowicz.cz/en/

Jirska, 3 | Prague Castle, Prague 119 00

Open from 10:00AM to 6:00PM

Lobkowicz Palace. Photo by <u>Chris Waits</u>

As soon as you are done touring the exhibitions of the palace, watch the midday concert- held at the concert hall (tickets may be purchased in combination with entrance to the Lobkowicz Palace). After an enjoyable morning at Lobkowicz Palace, walk over to **Mala Strana** (Small Side) – around a 10-15 minute walk, depending on your pace. **Mala Strana** is one of the most interesting neighborhoods in Prague, with quaint streets, Baroque architecture, and St. Thomas Church.

Before you explore the quaint streets of Mala Strana, stop over to **U Glaubicu** for a late lunch.

Try their beef goulash with bread (Hovezi Gulas v chlebu). Prices start at 180 CZK up for a meal. Take at least an hour or maybe a maximum of an hour and a half for lunch.

Open from 10:30AM-11:00PM

Malostranské náměstí 266/5 118 00 Praha 1 - Malá strana

http://www.restaurantuglaubicu.cz/en/welcome/

Mala Strana Prague. Photo by <u>Roman Boed</u>

Once refueled with lunch, continue exploring Mala Strana's streets, stores, and history. You can also check out the **Wallenstein Palace** – the seat of the Czech Senate, which used to be a palace in its own right, and was set to overshadow Prague Castle. You can actually tour the palace compound but the tours are only conducted in Czech and you'll need to email or phone in advance to reserve your place for the tour. If you can't go on the tour, go see the gardens, which are exquisite, with peacocks leisurely strolling the grounds. Allot around 30 minutes (or more) for the experience, and don't be afraid to sit and rest your tired feet for a while. You are in Prague, after all.

http://www.senat.cz/informace/pro_verejnost/in focentrum/index-eng.php?ke_dni=17.2.2014&O=9

Vadštejnské náměstí 4

Open from 10AM – 4PM, free of charge.

St Nicholas Church is a Baroque church also found in Mala Strana. You can enter the church and take advantage of a guided tour for 70 CZK, *available daily from 9AM – 5PM*. You can also attend one of the concerts if you arrive in season. Tickets go for 500 CZK. Check their website for exact dates and see if those concerts will coincide with their schedule. Allot a maximum of one hour if you took the tour.

http://www.stnicholas.cz/en/

Malostranské náměstí Praha 1 - Malá Strana

After exploring all the gems of Mala Strana, head to the **Petrin Lookout Tower** – built in 1891 as part of the Jubilee Exhibition, it is slightly smaller than the Eiffel Tower, but built with its Parisian counterpart as an inspiration. To get there from

Mala Strana, you'll need to ride a funicular railway that goes up to the top of **Petrin Hill**. Admission to the tower is 120 CZK, while the funicular costs the same as the public transportation prices (the bus/tram/metro tickets are valid on the funicular) and takes 4 minutes to get up the hill. You can climb the lookout tower – just be prepared for climbing the 200+ steps to get up to the top. You can also watch the sunset here, depends on the season you visit – summer days typically mean that the sun sets later while you will definitely be able to catch a sunset during the winter.

Prague Petřín Tower Steps. Photo by <u>Terrazzo</u>

Within the grounds, you can find exquisite landscaped gardens, a hall of mirrors, a church, and an observatory (additional charges may apply for every additional attraction entrance). There is also an in-house restaurant, *Nebozizek*, where you'll experience great views of the city. The restaurant is also accessible by the funicular. You can opt to have an early dinner here.

http://www.petrinska-rozhledna.cz/

Open between 10AM-10PM, depending on the month you go to (Nov-Feb: 10AM-6PM, March 10AM-8PM, April – September 10AM-10PM, October 10AM-8PM).

Prague seen from Letna Park. Photo by Roman Boed

If you still have the time and the energy, continue on to **Letná Park** (Letenské Sady) to see fantastic views of the Old Town from a different vantage point. From Mala Strana, you'd have to take a tram or metro, and it shouldn't take more than 30 minutes to get here. Take a relaxing walk where you'll get to see a large pendulum (called the

"Metronome") and views of Prague's many bridges (including Charles Bridge). If you get thirsty or want to celebrate your final day in Prague, opt for a visit to any nearby beer garden to sample delicious beers and end your day at the park.

http://www.prahazelena.cz/letenske-sady.html

7 WHERE TO HEAD OUT IN PRAGUE

M1 Lounge – a popular nightclub and ultra-lounge near the Old Town, there are themed nights and featured DJs that change daily, making it popular to clubbers with all sorts of music tastes. Best to reserve a table early to gain entry to the venue, and try the blue magic signature drink from the bar which comes with a blue glow cocktail stirrer.

Masná 705/1, 110 00 Praha, Czech Republic

Open from 9PM-4AM

http://www.m1lounge.com/

Bar and Books – originally from New York City, this popular cigar bar has made its way to various locations in Prague. Popular with expats and professionals, this discerning venue features whiskey seminars, charity events, and other themed events (sometimes, burlesque shows) depending on the schedule and the venue.

Manesova 1525/64, Praha 2, 120 00

Týnská 1053/19, 110 00 Praha 1-Staré Město,

Open from 5PM-3AM

http://www.barandbooks.cz/

Palac Akropolis – a popular music venue commonly visited by Prague residents, it hosts a varying number of international & local acts that vary day by day. It's literally where you can party or watch your favorite artists through the wee hours of the night, and do it all over again the next day.

Kubelíkova 1548/27, 130 00 Praha 3, Czech Republic

Open from 10AM-5:30AM

http://www.palacakropolis.cz/

Jazz Republic Prague – If you prefer Miles Davis to Miley Cyrus, then this is the place you need to check out. It may not be a clubbing place like most of the nightlife scene in Prague, but this is a great way to chill out and listen to some live jazz tunes. They also have an in-house bar and restaurant where you can just chill out and order a glass of wine.

28. října 1, 110 00 Praha 1, Czech Republic

Open from 5:00PM – 1:00AM

http://www.jazzrepublic.cz/

AAA Club Prague – If cabarets, gentlemen's club, and adult entertainment are what you're after, you can head to AAA.

Šrobárova 1988/6, 101 00 Praha 10,

Open from 7:00PM – 4:00AM

http://www.aaa-club.net/

Banco Casino – if your choice of nightlife is to possibly win more money, then a casino is a great place to do it. The banco casino is located between the Old & New Town of Prague, and is one of the oldest gambling venues in town. A dress code is followed on the premises so visit their website to learn restrictions.

Na Prikope 27, New Town, Prague 1

Open 24 hours.

http://banco-casino.cz/en/about-us/profile/

Bandol Winehouse – named after a French town and housed in the Cerny Slon Hotel, this wine bar offers various selections from the European, South Africa, and South American regions. You'll actually sit in a historic wine cellar, making for a more authentic experience.

Týnská ulička 629/1, 110 00

Open from 6PM – 1AM

http://www.hotelcernyslon.cz/en/prague-winehouse-bar-bandol/

8 PRAGUE LOCAL CUISINE

Trying different culinary dishes when you are traveling can be a highlight of your trip and a delight for your senses. Below, we list the famous dishes within the Czech Republic (which are shared throughout the entire country and not just Prague) and share some cooking schools if you want to learn how to make these dishes when you go home!

One of the main dishes of the Czech Republic involves *houskove knedlik*, which is a bread dumpling. The dough used for this delicacy is raised like your normal bread, but then it is boiled in hot water and sliced. It is normally served with beef *(svickova)*. Within Czech cuisine, you will find that the meat & potatoes (or dumpling) combination reigns supreme. In fact, the Czechs love their meat so much that vegetarians may encounter a limited selection of main courses to suit their needs.

The most famous Czech dish is the *vepro knedlozelo*. This savory dish is comprised of roasted pork with dumplings and sauerkraut. As you can tell by the ingredients, this dish is rather heavy, but it is very filling and delicious.

Sauerkraut *(kysla kapusta)* is commonly served as a side dish to most meat dishes (and other vegetable dishes) in the Czech Republic, so it's not just a German thing. Other common dishes widely available in the city which have a German influence include sausages (*klobasy*) and hotdogs (*parky*). Do try their fried cheese (*smažený sýr*) – deep fried cheese wrapped with breading, and the pork schnitzel (*smažený vepřový řízek*). Beef goulash *(hovězí guláš s knedlíkem)* is also widely available, as well as roasted duck (*kachna*) or roasted chicken (*kura*).

Another common side dish in the country includes potato salad *(brambotovy salat)* while dessert revolves around crepes *(palacinky)* and fruit dumplings (*ovocne knedlicky*), sweets filled with fruits and with poppy seeds. You'll be surprised at how frequently poppy seeds (*sulance*) are used in desserts within the region.

Of course, what is the Czech Republic culinary scene without a taste of their famous beers (*pivo*)? Their love for beer has gone as far as creating a *beer cheese*, which you should also try while in the country. But seriously, beer – they try to drink it with every dish, and the Czechs are the second largest consumers of beer in the world. The Pilsner beer actually originated from a town called "Plzen," so you'll be spoiled for choice for trying out these different varieties from various breweries.

Once you've tried the dishes, why not learn how to make them yourself? Below are some cooking schools you can enroll in for a class during your stay:

Chefparade – offering two types of classes, one for Czech cuisine (hands on) and another for a live cooking show (watch the chef do the job and you can do the tasting), you get to share a class with a

maximum 40 people and should take around 3-4 hours of your time.
http://www.chefparade.cz/cooking-for-tourists

Prague Culinary Academy – catered mostly for people renting apartments, the Academy provides a private tour where you learn to prepare the food directly in your home. This institute caters mostly to those staying for a longer term in Prague than short-term tourists.
http://www.pragueculinaryacademy.com/chef-at-home-en.html

9 WHERE TO EAT

Prague. Photo by <u>Jörg Schubert</u>

Czech cuisine is known for their wide assortment of meat and potato-based dishes, in particular, pork and beef. If you're a beef lover, try the goulash, a very hearty beef & potato stew that will fill you up for the day. If you're a pork lover, try the most famous Czech meal, vepro-knedlo-zelo. This is a combination of dumplings, roast pork, and sauerkraut, a combination that, when done right, is hard to beat.

For dessert, a great delicacy is parena buchta, a dumpling filled with jam and sprinkled with cinnamon and cocoa and glazed with butter.

Of course, Czech Republic is the land of great pilsner beer, but you can find any beer you desire on the streets of Prague, light or dark, sweet or bitter and creamy.

Prague itself has everything from hotdog street carts to five-star luxury restaurants, and also the home of two Michelin Star restaurants (Alcron & La Degustation Boheme Bourgeoise). While it mainly focuses on Czech and European cuisine, it also has a growing number of Asian restaurants, mainly Thai and Japanese.

Cheap Eats

Pod Slavinem – a well-known local place which gives out big portions for very affordable prices, prices range from 90 CZK up, and their website and menu is entirely in Czech so best to get someone to interpret them for you! You'll know that a restaurant is good if they mainly cater to the locals, and this place is without exception.

Try it out: Country Grub, a collection of bread, potato dumplings, potato pancakes, pork shoulder, smoked meat, sausage, and sauerkraut. Enough to feed an army!

Address: Svobodova 144/4

http://www.pod-slavinem.cz/

Open from 10am – 11 p.m.

Restaurace U Houdku – another great local place with good portions of meat and a wide selection of items, including vegetarian dishes, prices range from 80 CZK up

Try it out: Fried porkchop filled with ham and cheese.

Address: Bořivojova 693/110

http://www.uhoudku.websnadno.cz/

Open from 11am – Midnight

Giallo Rossa – a splendid pizzeria located in Old Town. The name of the restaurant refers to the supporters of the famous Italian Football (soccer) club, AS Roma. It is a non-smoking restaurant if you opt to dine in, so something to keep in mind. Prices range from 90 CZK up per meal.

Try it out: Pippo Pizza, a delicious mix of sour cream, mozzarella, pecorino cheese, boletus mushrooms and truffle oil.

Address: Jakubská 2

http://www.giallorossa.cz/pizza-restaurace/

Open from 11am – 11 p.m.

Mid-range options

Havelska Koruna – fast casual servings of traditional Czech food, with big portions and various dishes. You get a ticket when you come in, where all the consumed food is indicated, you pay the bill before you walk out of the restaurant. It's a bit of a fast food concept with a sit-down restaurant twist. There's also a year round winter garden that you can hang out in, and plenty of room to dine inside the restaurant. Prices range from 60 CZK up, depending on the small portions or meal you eat.

Try it out: Havel Chicken Schnitzel, named after the first Czech President.

Address: Havelska 21/23

https://www.facebook.com/centimetr

http://www.havelska-koruna.com/

Open from 11:30 am. – 11:30 p.m.

Restaurace Vltava – enjoy a relaxing meal and great views of the famous Vltava River! It seems small, but it is very close to the water so you are paying more for the ambiance. Prices on average range from 120 CZK up for an entrée.

Try it out: Trout curry with mushrooms and a glass of pilsner beer.

Address: Rasinovo Nabrezi 2084/1

http://www.restauracevltava.cz/menu

Open from 11 a.m. – 3 a.m.

Malostranska Beseda – the restaurant is only one part of this multi-layered establishment, which also includes a theater club, a café, and a cocktail bar. It is, however, the best part, with meals ranging from Czech cuisine to vegetarian, to European. There are a limited amount of seats and tables so get there early to secure a spot or reserve, if you can. Czech specialties range from 160 CZK up, with other cheaper options available.

Try it out: Roast Beef with creamy mushroom sauce and bread dumplings.

Address: Malostranské náměstí 35/21

http://www.malostranska-beseda.cz/en/restaurant/about/about-restaurant.html

Open from 11am – 11 p.m.

Deluxe Restaurants

Mlynec Restaurant – a sleek, modern restaurant with international flavor and great views of Charles Bridge, and has a formal setting. A sit down multi-course meal can cost around 800 CZK up. The restaurant is strictly non-smoking, and reservations are available on their website.

Try it out: West Bohemian Pork Belly with white cabbage, seared apple, and balsamic sauce.

Address: Novotného lávka 199/9

http://www.mlynec.cz/menu-en.htm

Open from 12pm – 3pm for lunch, 5:30 – 11:30 pm for dinner.

Terasa u Zlate Studne (Terrace in a Golden Barrel) – located on the 4th floor of boutique hotel Golden Well Hotel, the restaurant has fantastic views of Prague, and delicious international cuisine as well as unique twists on traditional Czech favorites. The building was built in 1528, and the restaurant was refurbished in 2008, giving an ambiance of a mix of old and new features. A two course business lunch meal can cost 700 CZK up, expect to pay more for dinner.

Try it out: Monk Fish with Homemade Spaghetti, flavored with Truffle Butter and Ossetra caviar.

Address: U Zlaté studně 166/4

http://www.terasauzlatestudne.cz/en/menu/a-la-carte/

Open from 7am – 11 am, and 12 p.m. – 11 p.m.

Coda Restaurant – exquisite fine dining, with a combination of Czech and International cuisine, located at the top floor of the Aria Hotel, and boasts of art deco interior and magnificent views from the terrace. A two course meal starts at 500 CZK, paying more for a three course experience. You can opt to get a cheaper ala cart menu as well. There are numerous wines and spirits available in the restaurant that you can also indulge in.

Try it out: Bohemian Wild Boar Goulash with Carlsbad dumplings, and finely grated fresh horseradish.

Address: Tržiště 368/9

http://www.codarestaurant.cz/en/our-menu/a-la-carte-menu/

Open from 7am – 11 p.m.

10 WHERE TO STAY

Budget-friendly accommodations

Florentina Boat- floating on the River Vltava, this hotel boat is definitely a unique experience – imagine looking out at the river when you wake up, but find that you are within a 5 minutes walk of the main attractions that Prague has to offer. Originally built in 1980 and was rebuilt starting 2008, there are 49 cabins and an in-house restaurant. The room prices range from 45 EUR up, with free buffet breakfast. They also offer unique cruises for your trip.

Dvořákovo nábřeží, 110 00 Praha 1, Czech Republic

http://www.florentinaboat.cz/en/accommodation/

Vitkov Hotel – renovated in 2007, this budget hotel is close to the Vitkov Monument, and is adjacent to Vitkov Park, which is not your typical Prague tourist attraction, making this location ideal for the more off the beaten path traveller who enjoys a taste of the real, quite Prague. This hotel has a lot more room choices suited for a larger number of guests in your party, but the downside is that you will need to take public transportation to get to the city center. They do offer free breakfast with every stay, prices start from 50 EUR up.

Koněvova 114, 130 00 Praha 3

http://www.hotel-vitkov.cz/

Hotel Koruna – A centrally located budget hotel, with 27 rooms, the Hotel Koruna was originally built in 1620, with the most recent renovation done in 2008. Rooms average around 45 EUR above a night and come with free breakfast. Though the hotel does not have any in-house restaurants or bars, there are numerous choices within walking distance from its front door.

Opatovická 168/16, 110 00 Praha 1

http://hotelkoruna.eu/en/

Mid-range enclaves

Sheraton Prague Charles Square – located in the heart of Wenceslas Square in Old Town, the Sheraton Prague has created a modern hotel with excellent amenities. It is notable for their French restaurant, Brasserie Delice, who offers a business lunch, which guarantees service within 30 minutes for a 2 course meal which you can enjoy with your colleagues. Prices start at 210 CZK ($9) and goes up to 390CZK ($15). They also have an in-house bar called the "Diamonds bar," where you can chill out and relax as you wind your day down in this pretty city. Prices range from 90 EUR above a night.

Address: Žitná 8, 120 00 Praha, Czech Republic

http://www.starwoodhotels.com/sheraton/property/overview/index.html?propertyID=3268

Chopin Hotel Prague City – Chopin Hotel's central location and comfortable amenities make it an excellent draw for both business travelers and families. It's close to Wenceslas Square, in the New Town, and the central railway station (Hlavní nádraží) is directly in front of the hotel. It has an in-house bar where you can pop in and order a drink or two from noon until midnight and a restaurant that is only open for breakfast. Prices range from 60 EUR up for a room.

Address: Opletalova 960/33, 110 00 Praha 1, Czech Republic

http://www.vi-hotels.com/en/chopin-prague

Domus Henrici Boutique Hotel – Located near Prague Castle, this hotel sits in a former 13th century house and is a great choice for anyone who loves history and affordability in the same package. Prices range from 54 EUR ($60 USD) up for a room, with special offers available for early bookings. There are only 8 rooms, each are spacious and are unlike other European hotels. While there is no in house restaurant, the hotel does serve complimentary breakfast every morning.

Address: Loretánská 11, 118 00 Praha 1, Czech Republic

http://www.domus-henrici.cz/

Deluxe accommodations

The Augustine Hotel – nestled in the heart of Old Town in a 700-year-old complex, made up of 7 separate buildings surrounding the cloisters of St Thomas Church & Monastery. This incredible hotel is a must for anyone seeking luxury in an unusual setting. A night here averages around $230 up. If you think about it, the price for this five-star hotel is not as steep other five stars around the world, considering the history that surrounds the property and its convenient location to most of the tourist areas you may want to see while you're visiting.

What used to be a refectory in the monastery has been converted to a bar, where guests can enjoy and try the hotel's selection of Archangel Cocktails. If you venture further, you might be able to see a cellar, which used to be the monks' old brewery; seems like even in the old days, monks loved their beer.

Address: Letenská 33/12, 118 00 Praha, Czech

Republic

http://www.augustinehotel.com/

Intercontinental Prague - An IHG hotel, with 372 rooms and 32 suites, the Intercontinental's location near Prague's Jewish Quarter affords sweeping views of the great city, especially when dining in its rooftop gourmet restaurant, Zlata Praha (Golden Prague). Average prices at the IC Prague range from $150 up, depending on the season. Sign up for the rewards before you check in so you can get free WiFi access throughout your stay.

Within the premises is a rooftop gourmet restaurant called "Zlata Praha." They are known for their Sunday brunch, from 1090-1290 CZK ($43-$51 USD). It allows you to stay from 11-5 and eat and drink all you can.

Address: Parizska 30, 110 00 Prague, Czech Republic

http://www.ihg.com/intercontinental/hotels/gb/en/prague/prgha/hoteldetail

Art Deco Imperial – An original and stunning hotel in the heart of Old Town, the Imperial's stained glass, high ceilings, and beautifully designed rooms make the Imperial a must visit for anyone wanting to get away from the traditional luxury model. It was originally built during 1913 to 1914 and boasts of an Art Deco exterior and is notable for its grand marble staircase in the lobby. It's also known for Café Imperial, a popular grand café house, previously frequented by Franz Kafka. Try their imperial cake!

Address: Na Poříčí 1072/15, 110 00 Praha, Czech Republic

http://www.hotel-imperial.cz/?lang=en

11 PRAGUE TRAVEL ESSENTIALS

Here are a few things to consider before you board the plane leaving your hometown to venture to Prague. Best to know these basic things to minimize culture shock and avoid standing out too much as a tourist.

Money

The main currency used in the country is the Czech Republic Koruna (CZK), even though the country is a part of the European Union. Some establishments dealing with tourists like hotels and restaurants accept the Euro, but best to just change your money to CZK when you step into the country. There are numerous money changers and banks to change your money in (but these charge commission), or you can withdraw from the ATM (which is the cheaper option). A credit card with an embedded chip is widely accepted. If your card does not have a chip, it may not work in some places (like train stations and self-service gas pumps – where only chip & pin cards are usually accepted).

Phone Calls

If someone wants to call your hotel from Prague, the country code of the country is +420 plus a 9 digit number, so if someone from the US needs to call your hotel (or you want to call an establishment in Prague), dial 011 420 *number* on your mobile or landline. (Example: 011 420 123456789)

If someone wants to call your hotel in Prague from Europe/globally, they will dial 00 420 *number* of your mobile or landline.

You may use your mobile phone if you travel to Prague but check if you have the appropriate roaming plan and if can be used in the Czech Republic. An emergency number to remember when using a Prague local number is 112 (for all emergencies, sort of like the 911 in the US or 999 in the UK).

Operating Hours and Sightseeing

Squares are normally open for 24 hours, but the major sites (like castles) & other small businesses, like shops, open between the hours of 9AM-10AM and close between 5PM-6PM.

Banks are open only on weekdays, between 9AM-5PM, with extended hours for currency exchange bureaus at the touristy areas. Sundays mean shorter operating hours for some establishments (opening later and closing earlier than usual days), and Mondays are when museums normally close. Good news though – most of the major tourist sites are open every day! In the summer, expect these sites to be open for an hour or two longer, allowing for more sightseeing, but note that Christmas and some major holidays like Easter can affect your schedule. There can be some establishments that are closed for those big holidays (banks for one are not open whenever there is a national holiday), so check the individual websites for more information or announcements of the establishment you are going to.

Tips

Generally speaking, the city is not of a tipping culture like America, but certain establishments round up your bill and the rest of the change is used as a tip. The common prices for tips range between 5-10%, or as stated, simply round up the bill. You normally tip taxi drivers, your restaurant server, tour guides (especially if you went on a free walking tour), or the street performers.

Restaurant Hours & Meal Times

If your hotel offers free breakfast, congratulations for nabbing one! Breakfast times vary per establishment, but they generally operate between 6AM-9AM. Other establishments may operate an hour earlier or later. Lunch is typically between 11AM-3PM while dinner can go between 7PM until as late as 11PM. Some restaurants close between the hours of 11PM-midnight, but you can still go to some gastro pubs which may stay open until the wee hours of the morning. Check the restaurant's website for the exact times as they may not always follow the norm.

12 PRAGUE TOP 20 THINGS TO DO

Prague is a hidden gem that it is impossible to not fall in love with. If you decide to visit, here's a list of the top 20 things that you can see or do in the city (in no particular order).

Old Town Square (Staroměstské náměstí) - Literally a square, it is full of life and is very busy. Within its cobblestoned streets, you can find a performer to watch or rest near the fountain area. It is also where you'll find our second and third attraction on the list.

Astronomical Clock Orloj – chimes on the hour, every hour – watch the walk of the apostles, a show of colourful figures. It can get crowded, though.

Old Town Hall - climb the tower, the underground area, and the historic halls of this 14th century gem. Open from 9-6pm.

http://www.prague.eu/en/object/places/188/old-town-hall-with-astronomical-clock-staromestska-radnice-s-orlojem?back=1

Prague Castle (Pražský hrad)– The biggest ancient castle complex in the world as per the Guinness World Book of records, this palace is absolutely big and also the place to buy an entrance ticket if you want to get inside the fifth attraction in this list. Grounds are open from 5AM to midnight.

https://www.hrad.cz/en/prague-castle/prague-castle-tourist-information/visit-of-prague-castle.shtml

St Vitus Cathedral – A Gothic cathedral built in 1344, popular the beauty of the frescos inside. Open 9-5PM.

http://www.katedralasvatehovita.cz/cs

Charles Bridge – A historic bridge with lots of statues, also comprising of 16 arches that connects the Old Town to Mala Strana. Open 24 hours.

Charles Bridge Boat Tour – Various companies offer trips along the Vltava River, ranging from an hour or more, various departure times, depending on the company.

http://www.praguesteamboats.com/small-river-cruise-through-prague

Mala Strana (*the small side*) – Historic district founded in 1257, known for the building's architecture.

Prague Zoo – A 58 acre compound, housing thousands of animals, also featuring trams and chair lifts for the children to ride and enjoy. Open from 9-6pm.

https://www.zoopraha.cz/en

Petrin Tower – Within the Mala Strana neighborhood, this tower was designed after the Eiffel Tower in France. You'll need to ride a funicular to get up the hill and see this attraction. Open from 10AM-10PM

http://www.petrinska-rozhledna.cz/

Letna Park – Large park that's home to the oldest carousel in Europe and to a beer garden.

http://www.prahazelena.cz/letenske-sady.html

Wallenstein Palace – home of the Czech Senate, home to a big garden (free of charge) and was built to rival Prague Castle. 9AM – 4PM.

http://www.senat.cz/informace/pro_verejnost/in focentrum/index.php?ke_dni=17.2.2014&O=9

Park Vysehrad - A historical fort with ruins of an ancient castle built on its grounds overlooking the Vltava River.

http://www.praha-vysehrad.cz/

Basilica of St Peter & St Paul – neo Geothic Church in Park Vysehrad, behind which is the Vysehrad cemetery, where many famous Czechs are buried.

http://www.kkvys.cz/category/budovy/

Lobkowicz Palace – A privately owned palace, home to a big art collection and a midday classic concert that's a definite must-see. 10AM-6PM http://lobkowicz-palace.com/cs/

Wenceslas Square – Square where lots of historic moments in Prague took place, with monuments and historic buildings surrounding it (such as Hotel Evropa)

National Theater – one of the most important cultural institutions in the Czech Republic which hosts various shows: from ballet, operas, and drama. Check their website for complete dates & hours of performance.

http://www.narodni-divadlo.cz/en

National Museum – A big museum comprising of many departments, from history, natural sciences, ethnography, and arts. Hours depend on which building you want to visit. Check the website for more details.

http://www.nm.cz/Visit-Us/

St Nicholas Church – Baroque Church built in the early 1700s – be sure to look at the dome and the sculptures on the interior part of the church (including an original pipe organ). Open 9AM – 5PM.

http://www.stnicholas.cz/en/

Old Jewish Cemetery – gravestones that are so close to each other, crammed in a small cemetery. The history is actually quite interesting – it was first used in the 15th century until it got too crowded and burials were stopped in 1787. It is not part of the normal tours, but definitely a great off the beaten path destination.

http://www.jewishmuseum.cz/en/info/visit/

CONCLUSION

Prague. Photo by <u>Thomas Depenbusch</u>

Prague is a wonderfully historic old town that one shouldn't miss when going to Europe, and it should definitely be a stop on your itinerary. Hopefully this small guide helped you plan your trip and gave you a background on the various spots that you can see (mostly for very affordable prices), where to eat, and ideas where you can rest your head after a long day of culture and exploration.

Enjoy your visit, however short or long it may be.

Three days may not be enough for you to enjoy the city, and you might just find yourself coming back again. There are also plenty of other places to see and discover within the Czech Republic, and Prague is just scratching the surface. Have fun, good luck, and as they say, Na shledanou (Goodbye)!

MORE FROM THIS AUTHOR

Below you'll find some of our other books that are popular on Amazon and Kindle as well. Alternatively, you can visit our author page on Amazon to see other work done by us.

3 Day Guide to Berlin: A 72-hour definitive guide on what to see, eat and enjoy in Berlin, Germany

3 Day Guide to Vienna: A 72-hour definitive guide on what to see, eat and enjoy in Vienna Austria

3 Day Guide to Santorini: A 72-hour definitive guide on what to see, eat and enjoy in Santorini Greece

3 Day Guide to Provence: A 72-hour definitive guide on what to see, eat and enjoy in Provence, France

3 Day Guide to Istanbul: A 72-hour definitive guide on what to see, eat and enjoy in Istanbul, Turkey

3 Day Guide to Budapest: A 72-hour Definitive Guide on What to See, Eat and Enjoy in Budapest, Hungary

3 Day Guide to Venice: A 72-hour Definitive Guide on What to See, Eat and Enjoy in Venice, Italy

Made in the USA
San Bernardino, CA
22 April 2016